Technology Timelines

SPACECRAFT

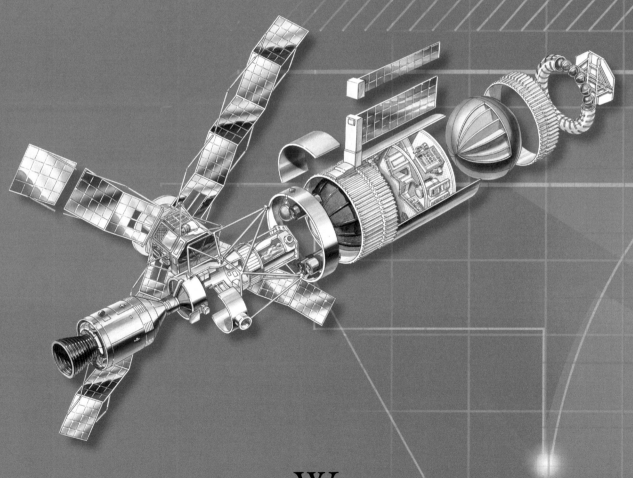

W
FRANKLIN WATTS
LONDON·SYDNEY

This edition first published in 2015
by Franklin Watts
338 Euston Road
London NW1 3BH

Franklin Watts Australia
Level 17/207 Kent Street
Sydney, NSW 2000

A CIP catalogue record for this book
is available from the British Library.

ISBN: 978-1-4451-3577-9

Dewey number: 623.7'49

Printed in China

Franklin Watts is a division of
Hachette Children's Books,
an Hachette UK company.
www.hachette.co.uk

Note to parents and teachers concerning
websites: In the book every effort has been
made by the Publishers to ensure that
websites are suitable for children, that they
are of the highest educational value, and that
they contain no inappropriate or offensive
material. However, because of the nature of
the Internet, it is impossible to guarantee that
the contents of these sites will not be altered.
We advise that Internet access is supervised
by a responsible adult.

Author: Tom Jackson
Designer: Lynne Lennon
Picture Researcher: Clare Newman
Children's Publisher: Anne O'Daly
Design Manager: Keith Davis
Editorial Director: Lindsey Lowe

Contents

Introduction

Space is not that far away. It starts at 100 km (62 miles) above the surface of Earth. However, fewer than 550 people have travelled into space and most have stayed close to our planet. The first humans flew into space in 1961, but the technology that got them there is hundreds of years old.

The first spaceman?

A Chinese legend tells the story of Wan Hu, who tied 47 large fireworks to a chair in the 1500s. He thought the rockets would power him into space. He boarded his rocket ship, lit the fuse and there was a big bang. Wan Hu and the chair were never seen again.

Fireworks

Spacecraft use rocket engines. These can work in the emptiness of space – unlike jet engines, which need a supply of air to burn their fuel. The first rockets were fireworks invented in China in the 800s. They were powered by exploding gunpowder.

<< A DIFFERENT VIEW >>

SCIENCE FICTION

Space travel was the subject of early science-fiction books. In 1869, American Edward Everett Hale's book *The Brick Moon* told the story of people living inside a brick space station.

War rockets

For centuries, Chinese armies used rockets as weapons. These 'Chinese arrows' were large fireworks designed to set an enemy camp alight. In the 1800s, the British Royal Navy began firing long-range metal rockets (right) from ships. These rockets were used to attack enemy ports.

Blast Off!

In the early 1900s, several inventors had a dream of exploring space aboard a rocket. However, the first spacecraft had no crew. They were flying bombs used during World War II (1939–1945).

Gunpowder rockets are not powerful enough to reach space. In the 1920s and 1930s engineers developed more powerful rockets that used liquid fuels. These rockets were first used to power fighter aircraft and as long-range missiles.

V2 missile

Germany's V2 rocket was designed to bomb targets 300 km (185 miles) away and the flight path took it high enough to reach space. A V2 rocket flew into space for the first time in 1944.

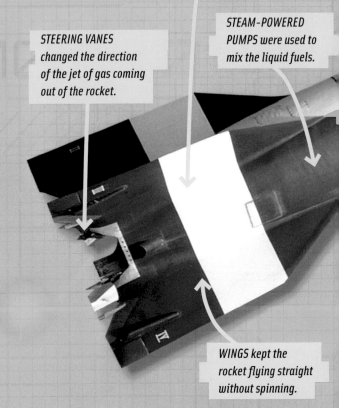

THE COMBUSTION CHAMBER, where the fuels burned, was at the base.

STEAM-POWERED PUMPS were used to mix the liquid fuels.

STEERING VANES changed the direction of the jet of gas coming out of the rocket.

WINGS kept the rocket flying straight without spinning.

TIMELINE

1903
Rocket theory
Konstantin Tsiolkovsky, a Russian teacher, (right) proposes using multi-stage rockets, which fire one after the other, to fly into space.

1926
Liquid fuel
US engineer Robert Goddard launches the first liquid-fuelled rocket. It is powered by a mixture of liquid oxygen and petrol.

LIQUID OXYGEN was stored in the lower tank.

THE UPPER FUEL TANK contained a mixture of alcohol and water.

RADIO RECEIVERS picked up guidance signals to keep the rocket on course.

THE WARHEAD was filled with high explosives, so the rocket blew up on impact.

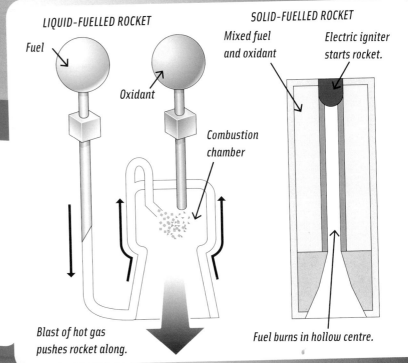

LIQUID-FUELLED ROCKET

Fuel

Oxidant

Combustion chamber

Blast of hot gas pushes rocket along.

SOLID-FUELLED ROCKET

Mixed fuel and oxidant

Electric igniter starts rocket.

Fuel burns in hollow centre.

« INSIDE OUT »

ROCKET ENGINES

A rocket is powered by a controlled explosion produced by mixing a fuel and oxidant and setting them alight. The fuels can be liquid or solid. The advantage of liquids is that the supply can be turned on and off to control speed.

1947
Flies in space
American scientists send fruit flies aboard a V2 into space. They are the first living things in space and return to Earth unharmed by their journey.

1949
Space monkey
Albert II, a rhesus monkey, flies to a height of 134 km (83 miles) above Earth in a V2 rocket launched from the United States. However, he dies in a crash landing.

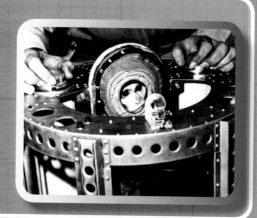

Into Orbit

In the 1950s, the world's most powerful countries competed to have the best space technology. Whoever won the 'Space Race' would have an advantage over everyone else.

After World War II, the world was dominated by two 'superpowers' – the Soviet Union (mostly made up of today's Russia) and the United States. These two countries led the Space Race for the next 50 years. In 1957, the Soviet Union won an early victory when it launched Sputnik 1, the first satellite.

Sputnik 1

This early spacecraft – its name means 'fellow traveller' – weighed 80 kg (about the same as an adult man) and it stayed in orbit for three months. It showed other countries that Soviet space technology was the best in the world.

FOUR RADIO ANTENNAE, for sending signals to Earth, stuck out of the back of the satellite.

EACH ANTENNA was nearly 3 m long.

RADIO SIGNALS were sent out in all directions.

TIMELINE

1950
Nuclear missile
The United States begins to develop rocket-powered missiles for carrying nuclear weapons.

1953
ICBMs
The Soviet Union begins to design intercontinental ballistic missiles (ICBMs), which can fly into space and then attack any point on Earth.

1957
Laika
A Russian dog called Laika is the first animal to orbit the Earth. She was sent in Sputnik 2, but there was no plan to bring her home and she died in space.

DETECTORS INSIDE recorded the temperature and pressure and sent the information to Earth.

NUCLEAR ROCKETS

In 1955 scientists began to research rockets powered by nuclear reactors. Their ideas did not work back then, but nuclear power might be used in huge spacecraft planned for travelling to Mars and other planets in the future.

THE SPHERE was made of aluminium, magnesium and titanium. The back half was shiny to reflect sunlight and make it easier for people to see from the ground.

1958

Explorer 1
The United States launches its first satellite, Explorer 1 (right). The same year NASA (National Aeronautics and Space Administration) is set up to run the American space programme.

EXPLORER 1
AMERICA'S FIRST EARTH SATELLITE
jpl   JET PROPULSION LABORATORY

1959

Astronauts
NASA test pilots flying the X-15 rocket-powered aeroplane reach the edge of space. They become the first people to become known as 'astronauts', meaning 'star sailors'.

Space Travellers

The next stage of the race to control space was to launch a person into orbit. In 1961, the Soviet space agency launched the first human into space.

A spacecraft that can carry a person has to have a life-support system that provides air and keeps the cabin at the right temperature. It also needs a landing system, so the pilot can get home safely.

Vostok 1

The first animals to return safely from space were Belka and Strelka, two Russian dogs who flew on Sputnik 5 in 1960. The following year, Yuri Gagarin became the first human to visit space aboard Vostok 1. He became a 'cosmonaut' – the Russian equivalent of 'astronaut'.

THE PILOT did not fly the spacecraft. It was all controlled from Earth.

THE 'VISOR' or navigation system allowed the pilot to see where he was.

THE SPHERICAL CAPSULE had a heat shield to protect it as it rushed through the air on re-entry to Earth's atmosphere.

TANKS contained oxygen for the cabin and fuel for the retro rocket.

TIMELINE

1961

Freedom 7
The first American in space is Alan Shepard. His Freedom 7 mission was a few weeks after Gagarin's. It lasted just 15 minutes.

1963

Space woman
The first woman in space is the Russian engineer Valentina Tereshkova. She spent nearly three days in orbit in June 1963.

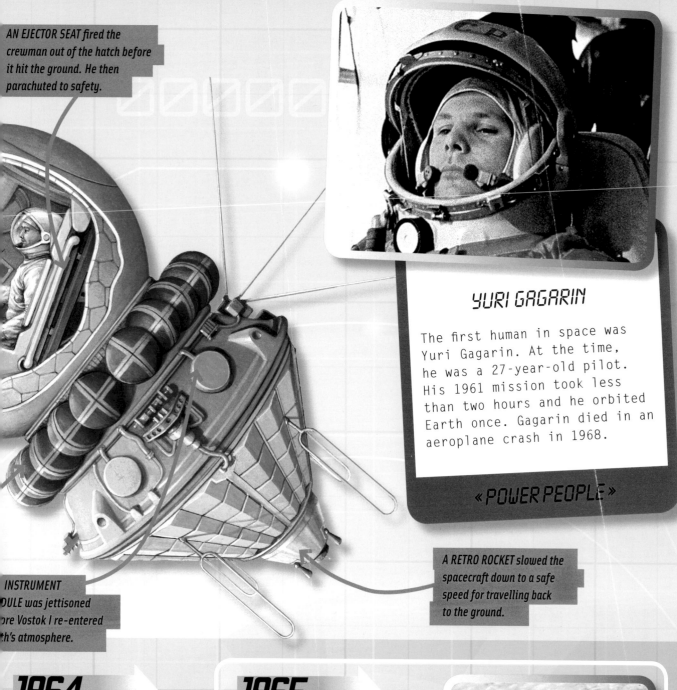

AN EJECTOR SEAT fired the crewman out of the hatch before it hit the ground. He then parachuted to safety.

YURI GAGARIN

The first human in space was Yuri Gagarin. At the time, he was a 27-year-old pilot. His 1961 mission took less than two hours and he orbited Earth once. Gagarin died in an aeroplane crash in 1968.

« POWER PEOPLE »

A RETRO ROCKET slowed the spacecraft down to a safe speed for travelling back to the ground.

INSTRUMENT
ODULE was jettisoned
re Vostok I re-entered
th's atmosphere.

1964
Bigger spacecraft
The Soviet Voskhod 1 is the first multiperson spacecraft – it has room for a crew of three. NASA also tests their two-man Gemini spacecraft.

1965
Space walking
Both US and Soviet spacemen make space walks for the first time. Russian Alexey Leonov was first, followed by American Ed White (right).

Moon Landings

In 1969, the United States space agency, NASA, landed astronauts on the Moon. Neil Armstrong was the first person to walk on the lunar surface.

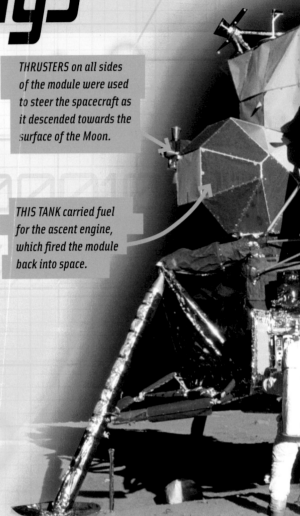

THRUSTERS on all sides of the module were used to steer the spacecraft as it descended towards the surface of the Moon.

THIS TANK carried fuel for the ascent engine, which fired the module back into space.

The mission to the Moon was called Project Apollo. It was the most ambitious space programme ever. Apollo spacecraft that reached the Moon would have to travel almost 1 million km (600,000 miles) on the journey there and back. Any Apollo spacecraft that touched down on the lunar surface would also have to launch back into space before returning to Earth – and keep the crew alive for two weeks. Neil Armstrong's famous mission was called Apollo 11.

Apollo Lunar Module

The Lunar Module was the part of the Apollo spacecraft that visited the surface of the Moon. The pilot flew it down to the surface from orbit. The lander had a small rocket booster for launching back into space.

TIMELINE

1966
Soft Landing
Luna 9, a remote-controlled lander launched by the Soviet Union, makes a soft landing on the Moon, the first time a spacecraft has touched down on another world.

1967
Saturn V
NASA begins testing the Saturn V (right), the tallest (111 m) and noisiest rocket ever made. It is designed to launch a crew of three to the Moon.

THE CREW OF TWO travelled inside the ascent stage cabin. Only this section returned to orbit.

THE DESCENT STAGE was used for landing. It was left behind on the Moon.

...IENTIFIC EQUIPMENT carried ...board was set up on the ...face of the Moon.

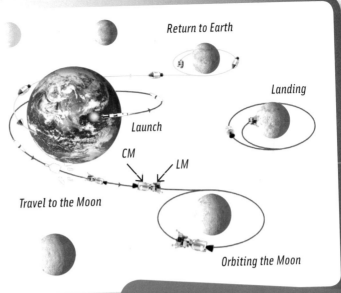

Return to Earth

Landing

Launch

CM

LM

Travel to the Moon

Orbiting the Moon

« INSIDE OUT »

MISSION SEQUENCE

A Saturn V rocket powered the spacecraft toward the Moon but only the Command Module (CM) and Lunar Module (LM) reached it. The CM stayed in orbit around the Moon while the LM landed on the surface. The LM then flew back to the CM, which the crew used to fly home in.

1968
Surveyor probes
Seven small unmanned probes (below) are sent to the Moon to check out landing sites for Apollo missions.

1970
Robot rover
The first remote-controlled space rover, the Soviet Lunokhod 1, begins a 10-month mission driving around on the Moon.

1971
Another planet
Mariner 9, launched by NASA, goes into orbit around Mars. It is the first spacecraft to orbit another planet.

Space Stations

In the 1970s, the first space stations were built. Their purpose was to see if crews could live and work in orbit for long periods of time.

The first space station was Salyut 1. It was launched in 1971 by the Soviet Union. That country put seven space stations into orbit. The last one that they launced in 1986, Mir, was their biggest and most advanced. NASA launched just one – Skylab – in 1973. Space stations are put into orbit by remote control. The crew arrive on a separate spacecraft.

Skylab

The American space station was built inside a converted fuel tank from a Saturn V rocket. Three crews lived there for a total of six months and performed scientific experiments.

A TELESCOPIC CAMERA was used to study the Sun. The crew had to make spacewalks to collect the photographic film.

THE CREW travelled to Skylab – and returned home – in an Apollo command module, like the ones used to reach the Moon.

THE DOCKING MODULE had hatches for two spacecraft to be able to join to the space station at the same time.

TIMELINE

1972

Into the asteroid belt
NASA's probe, Pioneer 10, is the first spacecraft to cross through the asteroid belt between Mars and Jupiter.

1974

Mercury flyby
Mariner 10 is the first spacecraft to visit the planet Mercury. No other probe will fly there until MESSENGER in 2008.

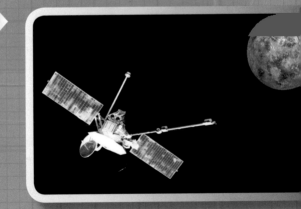

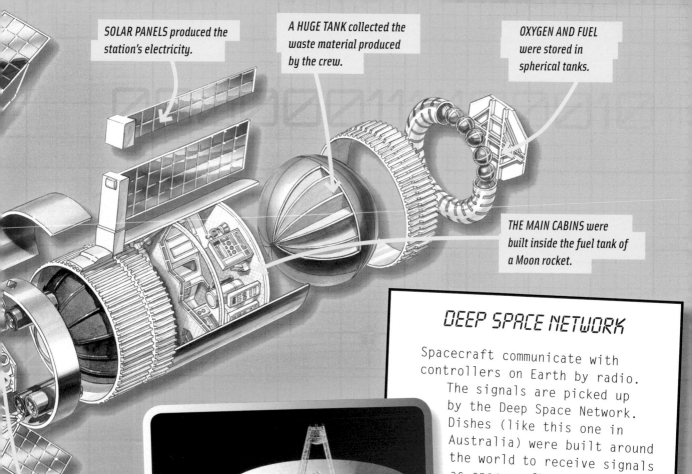

SOLAR PANELS produced the station's electricity.

A HUGE TANK collected the waste material produced by the crew.

OXYGEN AND FUEL were stored in spherical tanks.

THE MAIN CABINS were built inside the fuel tank of a Moon rocket.

E AIRLOCK allowed
e crew to travel in and
t of the space station.

DEEP SPACE NETWORK

Spacecraft communicate with controllers on Earth by radio. The signals are picked up by the Deep Space Network. Dishes (like this one in Australia) were built around the world to receive signals as spacecraft orbit around the planet.

« A DIFFERENT VIEW »

1975
Apollo-Soyuz
American and Soviet spacecraft dock with each other in orbit. Astronauts and cosmonauts meet in space for the first time.

1976
Viking landers
Two NASA landers touch down on Mars within months of each other. They send back the first colour photos from the surface of another planet and analyse the red soil.

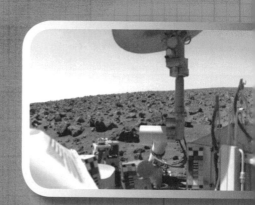

To the Planets

THE LONG DETECTOR picks the magnetic fields comin from planets.

Travelling to other planets takes several years, so unmanned space probes are sent to investigate first. Unlike a crewed spacecraft, these machines never come home.

In the 1960s, probes were sent to take a look at Venus and Mars, Earth's nearest neighbours. The first one to land successfully was Venera 7, a Soviet probe sent to Venus in 1970 – but the planet's extreme heat destroyed the probe in just 23 minutes. In 1977 NASA launched two Voyager probes on a 'Grand Tour' to the outer solar system.

TINY THRUSTERS are used to turn the probe in space.

Voyager probe

Voyager 2 took ten years to fly to Jupiter, Saturn, Uranus and Neptune. Voyager 1 left the solar system in 2013 and is still sending back signals from 20 billion km (12 billion miles) away.

A NUCLEAR POWER SUPPLY will keep the Voyager probes operating until at least 2020.

TIMELINE

1977

Enterprise

A prototype space shuttle, Enterprise, begins test flights (right). It has no rocket engines fitted.

1978

Navigation satellites

The first satellites (right) used in today's global positioning systems – or sat navs – are put into orbit. There are 32 in orbit today.

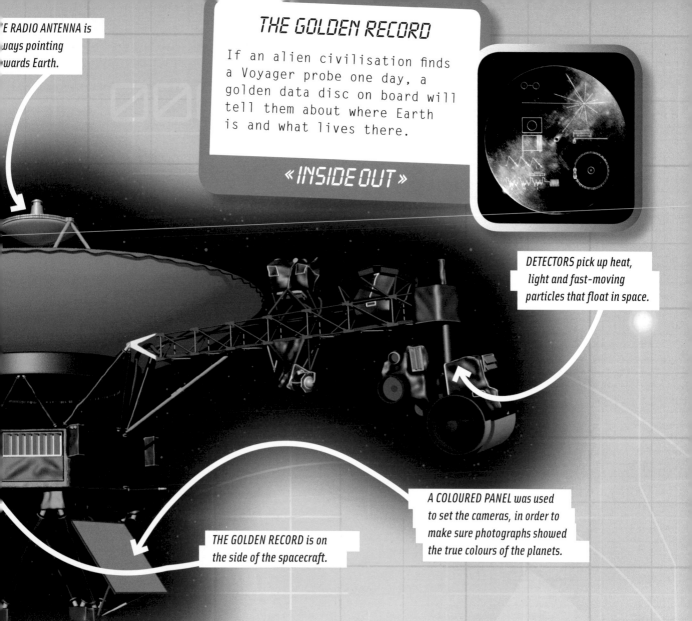

...E RADIO ANTENNA is ...ways pointing ...wards Earth.

DETECTORS pick up heat, light and fast-moving particles that float in space.

A COLOURED PANEL was used to set the cameras, in order to make sure photographs showed the true colours of the planets.

THE GOLDEN RECORD is on the side of the spacecraft.

1979
European rocket
The European Space Agency (ESA) launches its first rocket, Ariane 1, from a space centre in French Guiana, South America.

1980
Saturn close up
The Voyager 1 and 2 probes arrive at Saturn and send back pictures of its rings and moons (left).

A Space Plane

In 1981, NASA introduced a new form of spacecraft. The space shuttle was both powerful and reuseable, making human space flights easier and less expensive.

Before the space shuttle, only small parts of a spacecraft – the capsule carrying the crew – returned to Earth. The rest of it was burned up as it fell at huge speeds through the atmosphere. The space shuttle was a plane-shaped spacecraft that was tough enough to fly in and out of the atmosphere many times over.

Space shuttle orbiter

The space shuttle was the most powerful rocket system ever. It could carry 24 tonnes of cargo (two lorry loads), into space.

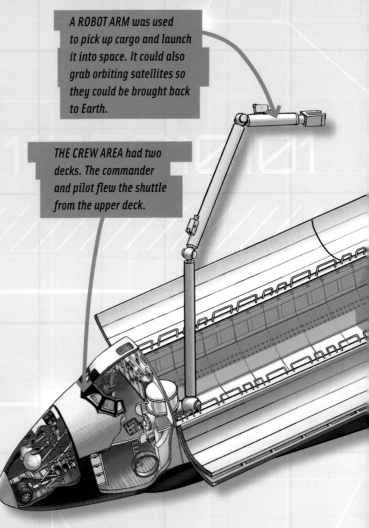

A ROBOT ARM was used to pick up cargo and launch it into space. It could also grab orbiting satellites so they could be brought back to Earth.

THE CREW AREA had two decks. The commander and pilot flew the shuttle from the upper deck.

TIMELINE

1984

Rocket pack

NASA astronaut Bruce Candless tests the MMU – Manned Maneuvering Unit. This jet pack is used for spacewalks and is not tethered to the spacecraft.

1986

Halley's comet

Five probes visit Halley's Comet as it swings by Earth. The ESA's Giotto gets the closest, taking this picture (right) of the lump of ice and rock.

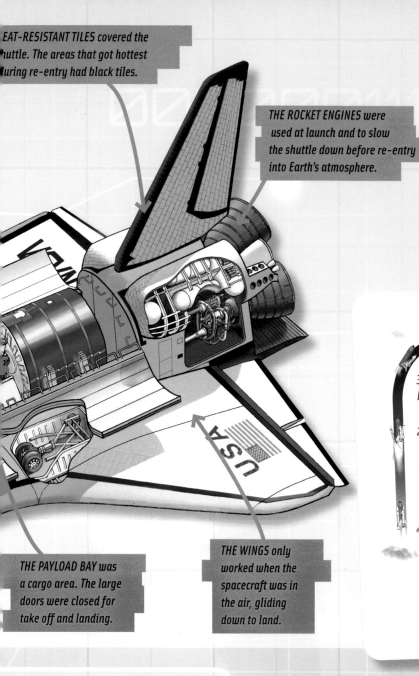

EAT-RESISTANT TILES covered the
huttle. The areas that got hottest
during re-entry had black tiles.

THE ROCKET ENGINES were
used at launch and to slow
the shuttle down before re-entry
into Earth's atmosphere.

THE PAYLOAD BAY was
a cargo area. The large
doors were closed for
take off and landing.

THE WINGS only
worked when the
spacecraft was in
the air, gliding
down to land.

« INSIDE OUT »

ROCKET POWER

A space shuttle landed
like a plane but took
off like a rocket. The
shuttle engines used so
much fuel for lift-off,
the fuel tank was bigger
than the spacecraft! Two
solid rocket boosters
(SRBs) also added power.

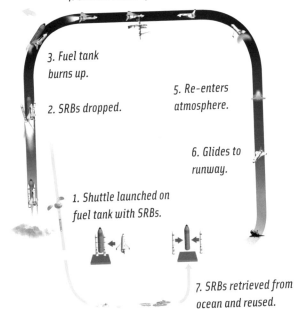

4. Shuttle orbits upside down.

3. Fuel tank
burns up.

2. SRBs dropped.

5. Re-enters
atmosphere.

6. Glides to
runway.

1. Shuttle launched on
fuel tank with SRBs.

7. SRBs retrieved from
ocean and reused.

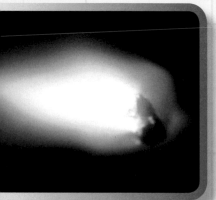

1989

Visiting Neptune

Voyager 2 is the first and
only spacecraft to reach
Neptune, the eighth and
most distant planet in the
solar system.

Space Telescope

Earth's atmosphere makes it harder for us to see out into space, even with a telescope. Putting scientific instruments into space gives us a much clearer view.

A DOOR at the end of the telescope is opened to let light in.

T he blanket of air that surrounds our planet blurs our view of light coming from distant stars and galaxies out in space – sometimes we cannot see anything at all. However, above the atmosphere, space telescopes and other observation equipment can detect objects that are too dim or too distant to be seen from Earth.

SOLAR PANELS on each side provide the electricity needed to power the telescope's computers.

The Hubble Space Telescope

This large reflecting telescope was launched in 1990. It uses mirrors to focus light from space into a powerful digital camera. The Hubble Space Telescope can see objects 13.2 billion light-years away.

THE NARROW SECTION of the satellite is a hollow tube that collects light from space.

TIMELINE

1990

Family portrait

Voyager 1, flying 6 billion km (3.7 billion miles) away, takes a photo of six planets at once: Venus, Earth, Jupiter, Saturn, Uranus and Neptune. Mars and Mercury were too small to see.

1992

Mapping Venus

The Magellan orbiter makes a map of the surface of Venus using radar (right). Before that, no one could see anything through the planet's thick white clouds.

RADIO TRANSMITTERS send digital pictures of everything the telescope sees down to Earth.

THE SHINY FOIL COVERING stops any light and heat from the Sun getting inside the sensitive spacecraft and spoiling the pictures.

THE MAIN MIRROR is inside the widest section. It is 240 cm across and can pick up light that is impossible to see with the human eye.

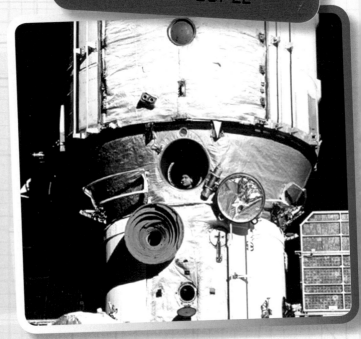

1995

Galileo probe

A probe is dropped into Jupiter's atmosphere. It falls for 58 minutes though the clouds, sending back information about the weather, before breaking apart.

1997

Sojourner

The Mars Pathfinder mission delivers Sojourner (left), a small six-wheeled rover, to the surface of Mars. It is the first rover to visit another planet.

Private Spacecraft

At first only the wealthiest governments could afford to send people into space. However, in 2004, a US company became the first to launch their own spacecraft.

In 1996, a competition was launched to build a reusable spacecraft that could fly into space – higher than 100 km (62 miles) – and then repeat the journey less than two weeks later. In 2004, a rocket plane called SpaceShipOne won the $10 million prize.

SpaceShipOne

The tiny 8.5 m long spacecraft was carried into the air under a jet aircraft. Then the spacecraft dropped clear and its rocket engine blasted it into space. It stayed in space for a few minutes before gliding down to land.

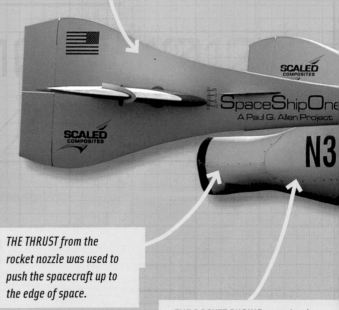

THE TAIL SECTIONS swivelled up to a vertical position to slow the spacecraft before it re-entered the atmosphere.

THE THRUST from the rocket nozzle was used to push the spacecraft up to the edge of space.

THE ROCKET ENGINE contained a solid rubbery fuel that burned when mixed with the liquid oxidiser (nitrous oxide).

TIMELINE

1998
Deep Space 1
The first ion-powered spacecraft is launched. It uses an electric field to create a jet of plasma (super-hot gas) that produces thrust.

2000
Expedition 1
The first crew arrives aboard the International Space Station (ISS). Since 2000 the station has been continuously crewed by people from around the world.

2003
Taikonaut
China launches Yang Liwei into orbit. Chinese space crew are known as taikonauts, meaning 'space sailors'.

ASTEROID LANDING

In 2001, the NEAR-Shoemaker spacecraft lands on Eros, an asteroid about the size of the Isle of Wight. It is the only spacecraft to touch down on an asteroid. It sent back information for 16 days.

A TANK of liquid nitrous oxide (the oxidiser) filled the middle of the spacecraft.

THE PILOT looked out of round portholes. These little windows are much stronger than a single, large windscreen.

THE PASSENGER CABIN had room for two people. In future, a larger version will take tourists into space.

2005

Landing on Titan

The ESA's Huygens lander parachutes to the surface of Titan, a large moon of Saturn. It finds rivers and lakes filled with petrol-like chemicals.

Mars Rovers

THE ENGINE uses the heat from radioactive fuel to generate electricity.

The next big milestone in space travel will be to send astronauts to Mars. To find out more, robotic rovers have already been sent to explore the planet's surface.

THE ROVER communicates with Earth using a powerful transmitter.

Landing a spacecraft on another planet is complicated. It cannot be done by remote control – it takes up to 24 minutes for a radio signal to arrive from Earth. So landers have to do it automatically. There have been several failed attempts to land on Mars. However, four rovers have arrived successfully. The latest one, Curiosity, is the largest and most advanced yet.

Curiosity

This rover is the size of a car. It arrived on Mars in 2012. It has a top speed of just 90 metres per hour. The instruments on board are looking for any signs that life once existed on Mars.

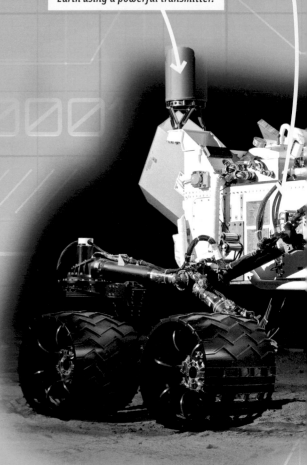

TIMELINE

2008
Ice on Mars
Phoenix, a NASA lander fitted with an excavator, digs into the Martian soil and finds crystals of ice, proving there is at least a little water on Mars.

2010
Space drone
The X-37, a remote-controlled space plane used for top secret missions by the US Air Force, makes its first flight. It can stay in space for months at a time.

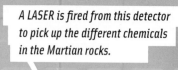
A LASER is fired from this detector to pick up the different chemicals in the Martian rocks.

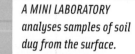
A MINI LABORATORY analyses samples of soil dug from the surface.

« INSIDE OUT »

SKY CRANE

The Curiosity Rover arrived on Mars via a rocket-powered 'sky crane' that lowered it gently to the ground on a 20 m cable. Once the rover was on the surface, the cable was cut and the sky crane was steered away to crash-land a safe distance away.

2012

Cargo ship

Dragon, an unmanned capsule taking cargo to the ISS (right), becomes the first privately owned spacecraft to go into orbit around Earth.

2013

Space music video

Canadian astronaut Chris Hadfield records a music video aboard the International Space Station (ISS). He sings 'Space Oddity' by David Bowie.

Living in Space

Space travel is no longer a special event, although only a few people get to do it. Every day there are between three and six people in space, working aboard the International Space Station (ISS).

The International Space Station is the largest spacecraft ever built. The amount of space inside is the same as the passenger cabin of a 747 jumbo jet. The ISS was built piece by piece, starting in 1998. Each section was launched separately and fitted together by astronauts during more than 100 spacewalks. The crew modules and other components were provided by many countries from around the world and the crews come from Russia, North America, Japan and Europe.

THE CREW sleep in this module. Their sleeping bags are tied to the walls so they do not float away.

LABORATORIES are used to perform experiments in weightlessness.

WEIGHTLESS TRAINING

All astronauts must learn to work while weightless. They practice inside a special aircraft, which flies in a way that makes people float around inside for a few minutes at a time. The strange floating feeling can make even the best flyers feel sick to start with.

« A DIFFERENT VIEW »

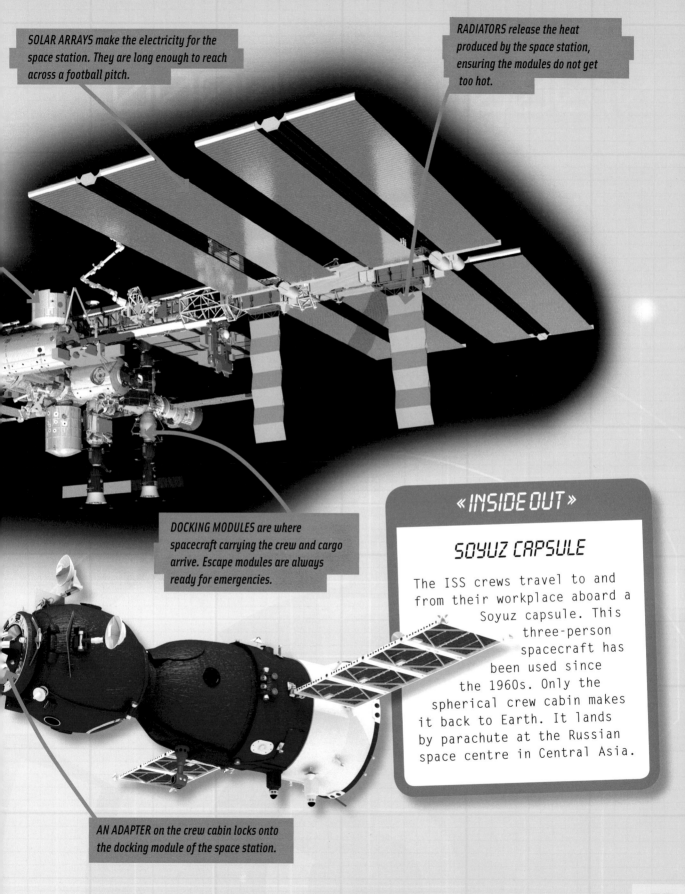

SOLAR ARRAYS make the electricity for the space station. They are long enough to reach across a football pitch.

RADIATORS release the heat produced by the space station, ensuring the modules do not get too hot.

DOCKING MODULES are where spacecraft carrying the crew and cargo arrive. Escape modules are always ready for emergencies.

AN ADAPTER on the crew cabin locks onto the docking module of the space station.

« INSIDE OUT »

SOYUZ CAPSULE

The ISS crews travel to and from their workplace aboard a Soyuz capsule. This three-person spacecraft has been used since the 1960s. Only the spherical crew cabin makes it back to Earth. It lands by parachute at the Russian space centre in Central Asia.

The Future in Space

The space engineers of the future have to fix two problems: how to make launching into space less expensive and how to send human crews on long missions to the planets.

Many space scientists hope that human explorers will visit Mars before 2050. It would need a massive spacecraft to be built in stages while in orbit. The journey to Mars would take months and a landing party would have to stay on the surface for a long time before it was possible to fly back to Earth. They would need to carry all their fuel, oxygen and food with them.

Space jet
The Sabre is an engine that works like both a jet and a rocket. One day it might be used to carry people and equipment into orbit for a lot less money than it costs today.

A NEW HOME?

Many billions of years in the future, the Sun will expand and destroy Earth. One place we could move to is Titan, a large moon of Jupiter. The bigger Sun could make this distant moon very much like Earth is today.

« A DIFFERENT VIEW »

Life on Mars
The air on Mars has no oxygen but it has plenty of carbon dioxide. This gas is used by Earth's plants to grow. The first people on Mars could grow their own food – and would not need to come home at all!

Star sailing

Rocket engines work well in space but all the fuel has to be carried up from Earth. Light sails are a space propulsion system that do not need fuel. They are huge mirrors the size of a couple of tennis courts that are pushed along by the light shining on them. The pushing force is only small, but over a long period light sails could reach huge speeds.

Looking under ice

Scientists think that life might exist in ice-covered oceans found on the moons of Jupiter and Saturn. Drilling probes are being planned to find out if there really is alien life out there.

Glossary

airlock The part of a spacecraft where air can be pumped in and out. This allows astronauts to move between space and the air-filled cabin.

antenna The part of a radio that picks up signals.

astronaut Meaning 'star sailor', astronaut is the US term for space traveller.

capsule An enclosed object. Small spacecraft are referred to as capsules.

cosmonaut Meaning 'universe sailor', cosmonaut is the Russian term for space traveller.

drone A flying machine that is piloted by remote control or steers automatically.

gravity The force that pulls objects down to Earth and also keeps spacecraft in orbit. To get into space, a rocket needs to push against gravity.

module A part of a larger object. Large spacecraft are made up from several modules.

multi-stage rocket The most powerful rockets are made from several smaller engines, or stages, that are fired in a particular sequence.

NASA The National Aeronautical and Space Administration, the US space agency.

nuclear reactor A container filled with radioactive fuel, which gives out heat that can be used to power a machine or make electricity.

orbit The path an object takes around a larger one. Earth orbits the Sun and the Moon orbits Earth. Most spacecraft are launched into orbit around Earth.

oxidant A material that makes a fuel burn. In car and jet engines the air is the oxidant. Rocket engines carry their own oxidant chemicals so that they work outside Earth's atmosphere.

radioactive When a material is unstable enough to break down and give out heat.

record A flat disc used to store information, most often music.

taikonaut A Chinese space traveller.

thrust The pushing force created by a rocket engine.

Further Resources

Books

Know it All: Space, Andrew Langley. Franklin Watts, 2014.

Out of This World: Rockets and Astronauts, Morris Jones. Young Reed, 2008.

Space Travel Guides, Giles Sparrow. Franklin Watts, 2013.

Space Exploration in our Solar System, Stephen S. Alison. CreateSpace, 2012.

Space Rockets for Kids, Philip Kebbell, 2013.

The Smithsonian Book of Air & Space Trivia. Smithsonian Books, 2014.

The Story of the Exploration of Space, Penny Clarke. Book House, 2007.

U.S. Human Spaceflight: A Record of Achievement, 1961-2006, NASA. CreateSpace, 2014.

Websites

http://www.nasa.gov
Take a look at the NASA web site. It has a kid's section and is filled with information about every space mission and spacecraft since 1958.

http://www.howstuffworks.com/space-shuttle.htm
A description of how NASA's space shuttle flew into space.

http://www.esa.int/esaKIDSen/
The European Space Agency's site devoted to kids.

http://www.bbc.co.uk/science/space/solarsystem/
Explore the Solar System with this BBC website.

http://science.nationalgeographic.com/science/space/space-exploration-timeline/
A timeline of space exploration from National Geographic.

Index